Traveling with Baggage:
A Guide for the Hesitant Hiker

Sarah D. Tiedemann

The information provided within this book is for general information purposes only. While I try to keep the information up to date and correct, there are no representations or warranties, expressed or implied, about the completeness, accuracy, reliability, suitability, or availability with respect to the information, advice, products, or services contained in this book for any purpose. I am not an expert or a medical doctor. This book is not intended to be a subsitute for the medical advice of a licensed physician. The reader should consult with their doctor in any matters relating to his/her health. Any use of this information is at your own risk.

New Boot Goofin Books, LLC
P.O. Box 523
Crosswicks, N.J. 08515

To Nick, my Alobar
Forever.

Thank You

Nick, first and foremost, without you, I'd likely not have anything to write about. Thank you for the countless nights spent editing and working through it. For a myriad of countless other reasons, thank you.

Mom and Dad, thank you for cultivating my love for reading and writing. You always told me that my best was always good enough, and with this advice I feel as though I've gotten much further than I would have otherwise.

Kirst, thanks for all of those late night calls and talks when I'm panicking. You're always the first one I call.

Laura & Shadis, you guys are the best! John, thank you for the badass logo!

Momma Bear, thank you for raising such an amazing son and being a source of strength for both of us.

Delfine and Mikey, thank you for encouraging me to come back to New Jersey. You told me I needed to go home to get my mana and that I'd be back some day. Those words have always stuck with me. Yours was the last conversation I had in Hawai'i, and one of my best memories. I needed that.

Jen and Lesley, thank you for being surrogate mothers to me for all of those years. I grew so much during my time spent with you both.

Ant, Laura, and Drew, thank you for your feedback.

Lastly, Papa Bear, thank you. You're sorely missed.

Contents

Forward

"You're an idiot" was my mantra as I put one foot in front of the other. I couldn't believe I had agreed to this hike. It was our first high mileage hike, and no matter how you prepare, you're bound to be caught off guard in one way or another. After 6.5 miles, I froze. A seemingly smooth, rocky roadblock was in my view. My hands started sweating, my breathing became labored, and I felt like throwing up. We were well above tree line and would have to scramble the whole way up. I couldn't imagine that this could come naturally to a person.

I stopped and sat down, trying to figure out the best route up the rock slide. Not wanting to stop after coming so far, I put one foot in front of the other, telling myself over and over, "you're an idiot" until I made it to the top of Mount Marcy, the highest peak in New York. At that point in time, I had been hiking frequently—but Mount Marcy was a game changer. I had never really pushed my mental or physical limits on the trail until that day. Despite being absolutely terrified, I was hooked.

In the following pages I will make fun of myself. Though it is my intent to be lighthearted, know that this is an incredibly personal account. As I was writing, I kept asking myself "do you *really* want everyone to know all of this? Is this a good idea?"

When I was first discussing this book with my husband, I was having a hard time finding what perspective I wanted to pursue. I couldn't decide if I would come from the place of my fear, my controlling nature, or my anxiety. Nick cleared the air immediately— why not all three? We joked about me exploring the trifecta of my neurosis...and I realized that is exactly what I should do. I find writing to be cathartic, but more importantly, I hope it will encourage you to get out of your comfort zone.

Most of this book will be about exploring the wilderness, but generalized travel is in the mix as well. We just happen to spend a lot of time outdoors during trips— for us, they go hand in hand.

The instances expressed herein are those when I've been at my worst. I have taken plenty of trips where I felt no fear. So, while I may seem a bit crazy, know that I'm not speaking in absolutes.

Part One:
A Little Background

My husband, Nick, and I are polar opposites. A lot of people use the term lightly, but trust me, it's the truest use of the word.

I grew up in an urban environment. When my parents first moved into the neighborhood, it was great for them. Little row homes where strung together on the block, anchored by a triangle shaped "park" (which in actuality was a grassy patch in an otherwise concrete jungle). This was a time when you actually became friendly with the people who lived in close proximity— we knew all of our neighbors. When you share walls, it's advantageous to get to know one another.

Anne, the neighborhood nazi, lived a few doors down. If she had been a man she would have had balls of steel. She was severe and unwavering. She did her part to keep the neighborhood nice and tidy and was always sweeping the sidewalks. She was fighting a losing battle but she didn't care. Every morning and afternoon, she'd hobble out of her home and get to work.

Evelyn, a schoolteacher, lived right next door. When my mother had an appointment or otherwise needed a babysitter, I'd go to Evelyn's. I loved being there. I was a leech with my mom— whenever she'd leave the house I would become inconsolable. When I went to kindergarten, I cried the whole first year. Going over to Evelyn's, however, was a welcome treat.

After spending time with her, at a very young age, I would think about what I'd like to do when I grew up. In those moments, I wanted to be a teacher. I would watch her grade papers with a red marker, taking mental notes. One memory of a particular visit to Evelyn's has stayed with me through the years. I had asked to use her bathroom to wash my hands. She only had a bar of soap at the sink and I recoiled. When she asked what the problem was, I told her that the dirt from my hands would stick to the bar. If there was any question about my obsessive tendencies, it was resolved in that moment, at the age of six. When I think back to that day, it's like watching a horror movie— you're yelling at the main character not to turn that corner.

Our neighbors on the other side were a handful. There were countless instances of absentee parenting, one of which involved a kitchen knife being used as an ice pick; another with a car running and a child in the driver's seat. I'll let your imagination run amok.

The street, directly behind us, whose residents' backyards butted up against ours, wasn't always off limits. I remember visiting a friend of my mother's— we had walked around the block, I was decked out in my plastic dress up heels (remember those?!), tip tapping all the way.

Things went on as normal for a long time. My mom would deliver Avon to the neighborhood ladies, carting her packages and I in a red Radio Flier. My dad taught me how to ride a bike outside of our house. I would sit on the porch with my sister's friend CiCi and we'd paint shells I had picked up from the Jersey Shore. Chiquita and I would play games, library mostly, and she'd help me with Hooked on Phonics.

As time wore on, the signs of a deteriorating neighborhood were slowly becoming apparent. In the midst of my parents trying to shield us from the big, bad world, I must have overheard conversations between them and the neighbors, and, in turn, started noticing unnerving things myself.

Almost every night, I would sleep in my parents' bedroom. When I was particularly young, I'd climb in bed between the two of them. As I grew older, they sanctioned me to the floor. It got to the point where they'd lay out a blanket for me in anticipation. I would grab my pillow in a sleepy haze and make my way to the narrow piece of floor between their bed and dresser. I'd always start the night off in my own bed but I'd almost always wake up on their floor.

My mom used to take us to visit with family over the summer. In the city, things always tend to get worse when the weather warms up, and Jersey's hot and humid summers are legendary. Crime certainly increases as temperature increases. We'd spend almost three straight months with family living near the Jersey Shore, only coming home occasionally to see my dad.

My sister, brother, and I were all enrolled in parochial school, even though it must have been a major financial hit to my parents. There was no way they would send us to the public schools in the area. I absolutely loved school and was an avid reader as a child. I would often retreat into the worlds I was reading about. I'd devour books about places far and wide, vowing that one day, I'd see them myself.

A new neighbor moved into where Evelyn used to live and brought with them an aggressive pit bull. I was no longer allowed in my backyard. A neighborhood teenager was attacked while sitting on her front stoop. I was no longer allowed to sit on the porch and people watch. I overheard a conversation about one of the neighbors getting into an altercation with a group of people, and one of them threw a lit cigarette into her stroller and burnt her baby. Anything beyond our front or back door was now out of the question, whether I was with an adult or not. The triangle park, where my brother used to play baseball, was off limits to him too. Everyone was moving out of the neighborhood and into the suburbs.

I noticed the locks on the basement door, which led to a short staircase on the outside of the house, accessible to anyone who bothered to try. I started thinking about how easy it would be for someone to break in. I would agonize over the weak points of entry in our home. I still have nightmares today, eighteen years later, of someone breaking in through the back door of the old house.

My inherent anxiety coupled with the neighborhood and subsequent sheltered upbringing led to my being a fearful person. Except for a short stint in my early adulthood, I have always been this way. I try my best to push it out of my mind but sometimes, when faced with fear or an uncomfortable situation, I recoil and return to my childhood self.

We knew that we needed to get out. Our family moved to a quaint suburb when I was eleven years old. I remember telling my parents that I was scared at night because it was too quiet. I couldn't sleep. Two weeks after our move out date, there was a drive by shooting on our old block. A neighbor my mom stayed friendly with had a small child at the time. He started having night terrors after the shooting. To say my parents were grateful that we left when we did would be a incredible understatement. And, in case you were wondering, Anne was the last hold out. She died in her home long after we moved out.

Even after we moved, I was still the same kid. My aunt once came to visit with my cousins and I was in my bedroom organizing. I would clean obsessively every other day and rearrange everything (including heavy furniture) about once a month. She asked me why I was inside cleaning and not outside playing with my cousins. The questioning made me feel guilty and introspective for a moment until the compulsion to continue took over. My dad will sometimes still mention how I wouldn't walk on cracks, would check locks over and over, and wash my hands excessively. As I've gotten older, I'm a world away from that girl. But, occasionally, remnants of my younger self will surface. It's like an itch that you scratch, and it feels really great for a minute, but then you find that you're itchier than before.

Though Nick and I grew up mere miles from one another, he had a completely different upbringing (and a different outlook on life). He led the typical outdoor-oriented boyhood. His father was an avid hunter who volunteered teaching the archery course for the N.J. Division of Fish, Game, and Wildlife for over a decade. He was constantly getting Nick and his siblings outside— hunting, fishing, camping, hiking, canoeing— literally everything a boy should do. His mother also joined in the fun— on her first bow hunt she snagged a nine point buck and made it in the local paper. She would always be the first one to the campsites, setting everything up for her exuberant family.

When prompted, Nick's accounts of his childhood are numerous (and equally horrifying):

> As a child, any opportunity he had to rip his clothes off was taken advantage of. He would run around the neighborhood stark naked, giving him his nickname "nature boy".

He started fires underneath his porch. In the same vein, he made his GI Joes go to war— specifically burning their plastic faces and limbs. We recently came across a bag of toys his dad had saved, and the carnage was *pretty* severe.

His mom would drop him off at summer camp. He would wait for her to pull away and walk home. He also hid from her so she wouldn't be able to take him to school.

He often went target shooting with his dad. Before he could even hold the .22 on his own, his dad would hold it up for him, while Nick would aim and pull the trigger.

Countless accidents, cuts, and bruises.

Snakes. So many snakes.

He stumbled upon (literally) a ground hornet's nest, proceeded to get stung numerous times, all while his dad was beating them off of him.

Though Nick grew up in a slightly better neighborhood than I did, he was by no means immune to the encroaching bad ones. He was jumped as a pre-teen where the thieves in training literally stole one dollar from him. One Halloween, him and his friends went trick or treating. One friend had his candy stolen. They went out again to recoup the supply. Again, his candy was stolen. This was apparently a tradition for the bad apples in the neighborhood because it happened several years in a row.

Nick doesn't seem to be scared of anything. Though he may have been slightly reckless in his youth, he has definitely toned it down in his adulthood. He takes calculated risks— but I still find them terrifying. He's a thrill seeking, adventurous man who I sometimes have trouble keeping up with. Despite being totally different, we fell in love.

We met through friends of friends when I was seventeen and it was amazing that we hadn't met sooner. We were friendly with the same people and his cousin is a good friend of mine. When we met, I had a ticket to Hawai'i already booked. We were inseparable for those few short months in between. The day before I was supposed to leave, I had a change of heart and decided to stay. The day of my flight, I had another and decided to leave. I left New Jersey on Valentine's Day (he'll never let me live that down).

Years passed as I built my life in Hawai'i. I never forgot about Nick, in fact, I dreamt about him often. I sent him a letter apologizing and letting him know I would be in Jersey for a visit and would love to meet up. He never called. I later found out that Nick was dating someone else at the time and his dad (who was always rooting for us) hid the letter so she wouldn't see it. Nick still has it.

Another year passed and I found myself in New Jersey again. I was at a diner with some friends, standing in line waiting to pay our bill. I glanced behind me and saw Nick waiting in line. I finished with the cashier and started to walk away. I was an absolute mess inside. My body was carrying me away but my mind was begging me to talk to him. As I was having that internal struggle, he grabbed my arm. We chatted for a couple of minutes and I told him I'd be in town for another week and that I'd love to see him. I stared at my phone that entire week. He never called.

About six months later, I was in my last class of the day when I got a text message. I didn't recognize the number but I knew it my heart it was him. That was the longest class I ever had. I ran out immediately afterwards and called him. I had been waiting on that call for years.

Coincidently, I had tickets to come home in four months and we spoke daily in the interim. Once my plane landed, I was terrified to call him to meet up. I knew once I did, my life was going to change and there would be hard decisions to make. I finally gave in and we spent my entire trip together. I went back to Hawai'i as planned. When I was on my way home from the airport, I realized that Hawai'i had lost its luster. I was ready to go home, this time, to New Jersey. When I got to my apartment, there were flowers waiting for me and I immediately started looking at flights. One week later, Nick and I were together again. Four years after that, we were married.

At the start of our relationship, we immediately started traveling together. Even though my upbringing was indoors (or perhaps because of this), I've grown to love everything about the wilderness. A relaxing vacation to me is running from place to place, logging as many awe inspiring locales and miles as I can. I knew it would be difficult for us to travel together but we went for it anyway. I'll tell you how I cope, but first things first. Why do I even bother?

Part Two:
Why?

Connecting to the earth in a different way:

On Travel: Think about the last time you thought about your surroundings. I mean, *really* thought about them and observed them consciously and intentionally. What we see in our daily life blends into the background. There's a reason why most car accidents occur within a couple of miles from your home…it's complacency. An easy way to become more aware is to change your surroundings. When we're thrust into an environment we're not used to, we become hyper aware and alert to everything that is going on around us. New surroundings sometimes present new outlooks.

On the Trail: This is pretty much a no brainer. Not all of us live in the country— most of us live in the suburbs or cities. I feel as though spending a day (or two or three) in the woods is enough to cure you of all the anxieties you suffer in your day to day life— no prescriptions needed. There have been studies that demonstrate being in the woods for even just one day can lower your cortisol levels for **weeks** after you return home. **Weeks!**

Connecting with people in a different, more genuine, way:

On Travel: In my day to day, I tend to see people without really seeing them and hear people without listening. It is far too easy to do. In fact, I think it's pretty normal. When you're traveling in strange places, you have to rely on other people. It's not usually a tangible reliance, but one of spirit and comfort. On the road it's easy to see that human connections are one of the most basic of needs. Nick and I savor meeting people on our travels— it gives you a quick glimpse into other peoples' lives, hearts, and minds. It teaches you tolerance. Plus, it's really fun to recount the stories of the people you meet:

Bear, the woman who, ironically, assured me that there were no bears in the woods of West Virginia (she totally lied).

Tanja, whose name we only know by her license plate, was acting as a pace car on a five hour drive. Her son in the back seat kept us entertained with hand written signs until we reached our next destination.

The Ohio Couple, who were camping with us at the same campground. We shared some beers and played cards all night. There were promises of keeping in touch, though no one ever exchanged contact information.

The California Couple, who, due to lack of phone service in Yosemite, were the first in the world to know my husband and I were engaged.

The Snowmobiling Crowd, who we shared a once in a lifetime experience with in Yellowstone. We spent hours together talking, laughing, and sharing our outdoor excursion with complete strangers.

On the Trail: There is a whole different feel on the trail than on the road. It's like going to a club for whatever hobby you're interested in. I'd say at least 90% of the people out there want to be there (the other 10% is reserved for bored kids and partners who had reluctantly agreed to go). It's easy to start conversations and meet people. In normal traveling experiences, you learn of the kindness of strangers, but on the trail, it's amplified. People are inherently good and genuine most of the time. Sometimes, you might just get a grunt out of someone. Other times, you end up walking three miles with them with aching knees and bleeding heels (I hope you stumble across this book, Gary!). One of our favorite parts of hiking is interacting with other people. When I lived in Hawai'i, I was hiking to a popular waterfall, Jackass Ginger. My hiking companion and I were stopped by an older Japanese man who barely spoke English (he was, we gathered, lost) and we walked with him the entire way to the waterfall without speaking to one another. He was all smiles, however, and meeting him certainly left a lasting impression on me. He had a bird call he was sounding off, and we all got excited when he received a response. No words were necessary to connect with one another. Though you might be shy and scared to do so, engage with people you meet on the trail. Compliment them, ask them questions about the trail or their gear, or even just a smile should do the trick.

Connecting with yourself in a genuine way:

On Travel: It allows you to get a grasp of what you really want out of life. Seeing so many different places and interacting with so many different people gives you a glimpse into your real self. All too often we're so caught up in what we're doing that we forget who we are. Travel is a good reminder of who we are, what we want, and how we're going to get there. It brings to light what really matters in life. I've had so many "ah ha!" moments on the road.

On the Trail: Being out in the woods breaks you down to your most fundamental level. It's a wonderful way to clear your head. There are numerous reasons why hiking is so good for you, both physically and mentally, but I believe the fact that you're exercising is one of the most important parts. I work in an office, and I've got to tell you— as soon as my feet hit the trail I feel infinitely better. Mental health professionals say that exercise is a great way to release some steam— and I'm inclined to agree.

The lack of distractions:

On Travel: This may sound counter-intuitive, but hear me out. I'm not talking about sensory distractions (which, after all, you're looking for— though I wouldn't necessarily qualify them as distractions), but distractions from your day to day life. There are only a few goals each day:

> Feed yourself.
> Find a place to sleep.
> Find a place to shower (maybe).
> Have fun.

This is how life is supposed to be: food, clothing, shelter, fun, and love. That's it. It's a great reminder that if we have those covered, we're doing something right.

On the Trail: Being outdoors provides me with a welcomed sensory input that actually makes sense. It's freeing to not be constantly bombarded with information that doesn't matter. My mind is quiet, I feel in the moment (without having to try). Again, there are only a few goals here:

> Keep fed and hydrated.
> Make it up the trail and back.
> Have fun.

Life is simple when we remove the things that don't matter. Unfortunately, we're slowly evolving into people who don't know how to be outside nor alone with ourselves. I once had an American Studies professor in Hawai'i who made a comment that really stuck with me. He was going on about "kids" he had seen on the bus that day. Nine out of ten had headphones in, engrossed in their devices. He commented that it was such a shame that people these days are so scared to be alone with themselves and their own thoughts. It's freeing (and healthy!) to focus on only one thing.

The feeling as though I'm getting something accomplished:

On Travel: If you're anything like me— you accomplish something, feel great about it for a day, then forget about it. In fact, after writing this book, I'm sure the novelty will wear off quite quickly. I'm goal oriented. I like having things to do. I like feeling as though I'm getting something done. Travel allows me to feel that way and the feeling lasts. I can't explain it, it doesn't even necessarily make sense to me, but it makes me feel great. It makes me feel like I'm living life as it should be led. It makes me feel like a cowboy in a western exploring new frontiers, and that's pretty badass. Nick and I track on a wall map where we've been and where we want to go, and it feels amazing to look at it and think of all the memories.

On the Trail: This certainly speaks for itself. Hiking up mountains that are inaccessible unless you put in work makes me feel awesome and as if I can do anything. There's a long list of mountains to climb and I intend on checking them off. How's that for getting something done?

It's just fun, plain and simple:

Once you remove all the major stressors and responsibilities from your life (even if for only a week), it is so much easier to relax and just have fun. Travel is fun; traversing new trails is fun. Plain and simple. I remember the first time I walked above tree line— it was like I was in another world. A major part of travel is expanding your horizons, and that's where most of the fun lies.

Time:

Time is never an issue on the road or the trail (unless you're checking on the sunset, of course). You're never worried about getting here or there, it just doesn't matter. I know not everyone can be less aware of the clock ticking— just try to keep in mind that you're doing this because you want to, there's no rush, and that you're flexible. After a couple of days in that "relax" mode, I'm sure you'll forget the last time you looked at your watch.

Something feels "off" when you return home:

It feels wrong to go back to day to day life when you've just had an amazing, perhaps life changing, experience. I find myself wondering what to do next. What could possibly top that awesome hike we just took, or that scenery we just laid eyes on? It's a strange emotion, but it means you're doing something right by fulfilling all of those travel dreams.

Part Three:
How?

I know my approach is wrong. I'll admit it—
I'm a train wreck when it comes to traveling. But here's
the thing— I do it anyway. I put myself through all of
this bullshit and I end up doing the things that make me
fearful anyway. Admitting to this makes me feel (and
sound) like a crazy person, however, I'm never regretful
that I faced my fears. I never think back and say to
myself "man, I wish I never did that". It has literally
never happened. The thing is, I never learn.
Professionals will tell you that you should keep
exposing yourself to your fears and eventually they
won't scare you. In my experience, they're wrong. But I
still keep coming back for more, so why bother with the
fear? I'm going to go anyway, so why bother going
kicking and screaming and instead just give in to the
experience? Isn't that what it's all about? The
opportunity to free yourself from the confines of day to
day life? To grow?

I like to pretend that I'm someone else,
someone more confident and capable. You should try it
sometime. No one knows who you are, you're
completely removed from everything you know and are
comfortable with— there's no danger in letting loose.
It's like calling on an alter ego, and it will serve you well
to do so. Practicing this has actually increased my
confidence in my daily life. *Fake it till you make it.*

Look, I'm no expert. I still have anxiety. I'm still
scared. But what separates me from the other yellow-
bellied folks is that I do it anyway. I *do* have some
coping skills otherwise I would never leave the house.

It's imperative that you realize that anxiety is
closely tied to lack of confidence. Once you address
this, most fear will fall away. Be confident! Know that
you're good. Pretend if you have to— pretty soon it'll

become who you are.

Well, here it is— my fears, my traveling style, and my tips for letting go.

I.
The Preparation

Finding flights or driving routes: I will never book through a third party travel website ever again. First, the price difference is usually minimal. Second, I don't like booking cars, flights, and hotels all at the same time—too much can change before a trip to make it worth the supposed savings. Third, we had an awful experience a few years ago with a popular travel website. We booked our flights months out, reserved a car, and booked only our first night at a hotel. I had gotten a few emails from the website changing the flight times, but last I checked (on the way to the airport), it was still on for the original time. We arrive at the airport and there is no one in the terminal— not even a clerk at the airline desk. Though at that point it was glaringly obvious, we finally found someone who said that the flight had left hours earlier. I immediately called customer service for the website and they basically told me tough shit— I should have checked the airline's website for any changes. They also noted that they sent out an email an hour before (three hours after the flight took off!) advising of this change. I never received that email, not that it would have made any difference. The clerk at the airport was a lifesaver. She was able to get us on another flight that was slated to leave in an hour. She advised us not to tell anyone we were previously booked on her airline. It ended up being a million times better— we had a nonstop flight (with no fare increase) and barely lost any time on our trip (though no thanks to the website we originally booked with). So, long story short, no travel websites for me. They were incredibly unhelpful and a huge disappointment. I will only book directly with airlines from now on. Often times they have the best prices and the risk of getting screwed are very low.

Speaking of airlines, I'm really only comfortable flying with a handful of them. I check aviation accidents and incident reports to make sure my choices are up to date. I've got this part pretty much on lockdown. The hardest part is figuring out what our flight time should be (to minimize traffic to and in the airport), what time we'll be arriving at our destination (to minimize lost vacation time), and what days are the best to fly out on (to minimize costs).

When we're driving to our destination, I go through all the possible routes and pick the ones that scare me the least. I surely try, but sometimes, I can't avoid the N.J. Turnpike, Garden State Parkway, or the dreaded Interstate 95 in Connecticut. Horrible traffic, even worse drivers, and an endless slew of accidents make these my least favorite routes. I'm sure you have your own stories— but have you ever seen a gang of teenagers on bicycles, weaving in and out of HIGHWAY traffic (right before the George Washington Bridge?!) while passing a joint between the four of them, or a van that caught fire with its' passenger nonchalantly standing next to it, or several accidents all on the same highway?

Finding lodging: Aside from incessant worrying, this is what takes the most time for me. It's incredibly difficult to find the perfect place (for me) to stay, in our price range, with good reviews, and close to the places we want to see. I will literally spend hours searching and it's mostly because of bedbugs. This isn't an unreasonable fear— they are super prevalent and we've gotten them before. On Trip Advisor, I use the search function on my browser to see if "bedbugs" were mentioned in every.single.page of reviews. Getting bedbugs and the subsequent shit storm that followed certainly made me change the way I look for lodging. Thereafter, I'll use Google Street View to take a look around the neighborhood of the hotel in question. We once booked a hotel in Denver but it turned out to be in an industrial area miles away from the city center. We won't be making that mistake again. After that, I'll cross reference other travel review websites. The hotel needs to have free WiFi and parking (it's insane how a hotel can charge for these things when you're paying upwards of $100 a night to stay there). Lastly, I'll look for coupons or deals because we all know lodging is usually the most expensive part of any trip.

On big trips, I don't like to camp (it's way too much to think about and pack) and hostels just aren't for me even though they'd probably save us money. I feel vulnerable when I'm sleeping and being particular about my sleeping quarters precludes this as an option. That said, I have tried Couch Surfing. I wanted desperately to go on a trip I just flat out didn't have the money for. Nick and I chose the least suspicious, most warm, and seemingly normal person we could find. We had a backup plan in case things were sketchy once we arrived. We would leave all of our belongings in the car, check out the house, suss out the host, and if we weren't comfortable we would say we needed to get food and just leave. Luckily, we had an amazing hostess, Sarah, who was truly fantastic. I'm so happy that we were able to have our first Couch Surfing experience with her. We talked for hours about all kinds of things and even took a hike together. We weren't murdered, we made a new friend, and we didn't pay a cent (except for a post hike meal and beer). Our next Couch Surfing experience came as a recommendation from Sarah when we were driving to Missouri. Hayley was an amazing hostess as well (she let us stay with her at the last minute on our return trip too!) and we really enjoyed her company. We had a ton of changes and life events going on at the time of the trip and it was a really emotional one for us. The sense of normalcy that staying in someone's home (rather than a hotel) provides while on the road is incredibly comforting. It's a really great community (if you are cautious and use common sense) and I highly recommend it to everyone.

Finding activities/hikes: I'm okay with a brisk hike in the woods. Nick's better when he's "on a mountaintop breaking a trail through fresh snow". Because our personalities and travel styles are so different, we have very interesting, passionate discussions when it comes to planning.

When we first start to plan, we have a general idea of where we want to go, but as far as activities are concerned, we'll make separate lists on our own time. When we bring our lists to the table and start to discuss them, our exchange typically follows this format:

Playful Banter. We will flat out ignore what the other says. Nick will say he doesn't want to do *x* and I'll say that it's settled and we're doing *x* then, and that I'm glad he agrees that it is a good idea. We have always been good at banter and travel planning is no exception. There is truth in jest, however, so the exchange continues:

Guilt. We'll claim that one of us doesn't want the other to have any fun. We're still kind of joking.

Pleading. Nick will ask me to just get over my fear of whatever it is that he's trying to do. I will ask him to get over me not wanting to.

Defeat. The conversation usually ends for the night with one of us exasperatingly saying that we won't do anything at all because we can't come to an agreement. We agree to revisit the discussion later.

After we sleep on it, we'll come back together the following day, at which point we've both waned in our absolute must do (or not do) criteria. This isn't something we'll do all in one day— we'll keep coming back and discussing our options. It gives us both time to think about what we really want to do and figure it out with as little pressure or stress as possible. During this process, we'll look at countless pictures, videos of the trail, elevation information (this is key—you need to know what you're in for. A three mile hike can be infinitely more difficult than an eight mile hike).

Lists: I absolutely love them. They bring such simplicity into everyday life— a couple of sheets of paper and boom—everything suddenly makes sense. Outdoor excursions and traveling allow me to write a ton of lists, and I savor every minute of it (until I actually have to do something about them).

Lists of lists:

> Things to do now
> Things to pack now
> Things we need to buy
> Things to do and pack weeks in advance
> Things to do and pack five days prior
> Things to do and pack on the day of departure

Addresses and phone numbers:

> All trailhead addresses, maps, and routes. I will look through as many trail reports as I can get my hands on. I want to be prepared to go out there and I want to know (to a certain extent) what to expect.
>
> All campgrounds/lodging (whether booked yet or not).
>
> All emergency numbers for rangers in the area. If you haven't heard or bothered to think about it, only dial 911 if you are unsure of these numbers. It is better to call someone who knows the area and the trails (and might be able to tell exactly where you are based on something seemingly meaningless) than to call a 911 operator who will have no idea what you're talking about. I'll plug these into our phones, on our itinerary, and on a sticky note in each of our pockets.
>
> A list of our emergency contacts and health conditions in each of our backpacks.

Plans and back up plans of things we want to do with corresponding contact information. I'll have different combinations for different days. This allows us to be flexible— if one of us isn't feeling well, we want a lazy day, or we're feeling super energetic and adventurous—we have options. We've done enough scrambling on trips trying to figure out what we should do. Back up plans allow us to minimize lost time and stress. There's no "well what do *you* feel like doing?" for hours on end. We've been there and it's not fun.

Further lists:

I compile about two dozen pieces of handwritten notes, including flight times, numbers, and airport codes.

Put everything together in a rough draft.

Rewrite in a shiny, typed (or beautifully handwritten) package complete with stamps, stickers, and ribbon. I'd even give it a wax seal if I had the supplies.

Give copies of the itinerary to Nick's sister Laura, his mom, and my mom with explicit instructions that if they don't hear from us by a certain time to send in the cavalry.

The first aid/survival kit: Nick and I always have disagreements over what we're going to bring in our first aid kits. Usually, I'm able to sneak in a few extra items I think are important. A couple of years back I expanded out first aid kits, and if I had it my way, every single one of the following items would go on every trip with us (sit tight, there's a lot!).

> Band aids (Nick claims they're useless. He's tried only bringing super glue and duct tape. Band aids are easy to hide. Gotcha, Nick!)

> Quik Clot (these will stop bleeding in the event of a major accident. Nick was not happy when I compiled my kit—these cost over $20 a piece. I bought two.)

> Duct tape

> Super Glue

> Lighter

> Storm proof matches (REI makes these and they are amazing. Watch a video— you can literally soak them in water and find that they are still lit.)

> Magnesium fire starter

> Ace bandage

> Needle and thread

Benadryl (a lot of it, in case of an allergic reaction.)

Tylenol

Aspirin

Tums (a shit ton. I get awful heartburn, especially when I'm active.)

Glucose tablets (for sugar lows.)

Some sort of backup filtration (we have filters on our pack bladders.)

Wilderness first aid book (though I'm sure that in the event of an emergency, I wouldn't have time to flip through the pages, it still makes me feel better.)

CPR instructions (again, see above. We're both certified. I doubt we'll forget what to do.)

CPR masks (Nick put the kibosh on that as soon as the package came. They've never been on a trip.)

Instructions on encountering bear and mountain lion (for nighttime campfire reading? I don't know what I expect. Maybe I could ask the massive mammal to hang on a second while I look up what to do. I guess I fear I'll forget in the heat of the moment.)

Space blanket (for two :)

Ponchos

Signal mirror

Firecrackers (to scare the bears!)

Tweezers

Scissors

Safety pins

Pen and paper

Sunscreen and lip balm

Feminine products

Toilet paper

Moleskin (for blister protection.)

Extra knife (in addition to the ones already on our person.)

Gear/supplies check: Most of the following is only done once at the beginning of every season:

Change batteries in headlamps, lanterns, and flashlights

Charge batteries in phones and cameras

Double check that all memory cards are empty (even though I already know they are.)

Check expiration date of bear maces: yes, plural. I have three. Funny story about the bear mace— after pulling into the driveway after an eight hour car ride, I decided to pull only my toiletry bag out of the trunk and turn in for the night. The bag got caught on the bear mace and somehow caused it to discharge while my face was in the trunk. It burned like hell. I "washed" my face with milk in the sink for about twenty minutes. This is highly unlikely to happen to you as there is a pin in place to prevent accidental discharges, but, you know, Murphy's Law. As a side note, however, it's an extremely important addition to anyone's gear cache. Thankfully, I've never had to use it on a bear.

Test personal locator beacon (a recent wish list purchase! I was so excited, $225 and it was half off! Better to have it and not need it, right?)

Check to make sure fog horns are still working (I carry around mini ones to scare wildlife or get someone's attention. They're made for boats and are super loud and effective.)

Check expiration of all medications.

Check and double check that I have my medic alert bracelet (in the event that Nick isn't around, it tells medics things they probably should know. It makes no sense, however, as I never wear it in my daily life, where I'm much more likely to need it.)

Make sure our voice over internet app is working properly. If you don't have one yet, download it. It's free and has allowed us to make calls over the internet (for when we don't have cellular service but there is WiFi). It's a great way to stay in touch with family over the course of your trips. We wouldn't have been able to make ANY calls in Wyoming until we reached Jackson Hole, eight hours from our starting point. It could prove to be a lifesaver some day.

Actual packing (eek!): As much as I love packing lists and crossing out to dos, I absolutely hate packing. I always think I'll forget something and it drives me crazy. It takes entirely too long to accomplish. I'll usually leave this to Nick but when he takes the reins I am pretty uncomfortable. He'll surely forget something and in my head it'll be a critical item. If we're just going somewhere wherein we won't need any hiking or camping gear, I relax a bit. But, for instance, on a trip to Hawai'i, we needed two weeks worth of clothing, hiking gear, camping gear, food, and supplies for three days on the trail. I was packing literally months ahead.

After everything is done, I'll begin to anxiously check my lists, check my packing piles, and check the weather. I will go through things incessantly until we depart.

Relief!

Realize that you can't control every situation: We have no control. We'd all like to think we do but we most certainly don't. It can be terrifying at times, but if you look at it in a positive light, it can be very freeing. You have no control! You can plan and plan away but sometimes things just don't go your way. On our Hawai'i trip, Nick and I were ill for the final five days of our two week stay. Nick had gotten sick first, starting with a fever and cough, which progressed into swollen lymph nodes in his groin. We were so freaked out that we spent the evening in the emergency room to make sure nothing more sinister was going on. We were confined to a hotel room for the remainder of our trip. It definitely pained me to do so, but there was absolutely nothing I could do about it. We laughed and resolved to go back. Forcing things to happen when you don't accept misfortune can quickly become dangerous. Sometimes you just have to give in.

Be flexible: There's no reason not to bend. You can either be uncomfortable and stressed out or accept it and find a solution. It will make your life a lot easier. And sometimes, things will turn out better than you could have hoped for. Had we not gotten bedbugs in Colorado, we would have never snowmobiled in Yellowstone. Although it was slightly terrifying to weave through herds of buffalo, I'd say that was a decent payoff.

Sometimes, not being flexible means you miss out on great opportunities. Upon arriving in a small town in the Adirondacks, Nick wanted to stop at a little eatery to grab some dinner. Having our schedule "all figured out", I wanted to check into the bed and breakfast before we ate. We checked in and made our way back to the restaurant. The boss himself, Bruce Springsteen, had just left after having dinner, sharing brews, and taking photographs with fellow patrons. My heart sunk. As a Jerseyan, it was a serious blow. As I cursed myself, I remembered seeing the motorcycles outside of the restaurant when we passed it the first time. We definitely would have met him if we had stopped when Nick wanted to.

Find a good ratio: I still haven't gotten this one down. You *should* be prepared to travel or go into the woods. It would otherwise be irresponsible to yourself, the people traveling with you, and those who will have to come and save your ass. BUT you have to learn to put a cap on it and not obsess too much. As far as packing is concerned, if you arrive at your destination without an item, it's almost always just a matter of price. Most likely, you can buy anything you've forgotten.

Realize that you are an intrepid traveler: Think back on trying times. You can (and have!) handled anything that came your way. It also helps to think of past explorers and travelers. They were the ones contending with real danger. Your travels are a walk in the park comparatively.

Statistics (usually): This is what most people look to, and it works most of the time. You know, like you're much more likely to die on the way to the airport, rather than in a plane crash (and that's supposed to be comforting?!). One thing is going to seem more harrowing than the next. Use this tactic at your own risk.

Trust your traveling partner: Nick isn't scared of much, and I look to him to quell my fears. Sometimes, I find it infuriating because I can't imagine why a certain thing doesn't scare him; other times it's a major source of strength. I know I usually don't have much to fear when he's nonchalant about it.

Work out worse case scenarios out loud: Do it with someone else in the room and have them give you feedback. When you're overanalyzing something you're scared about, it usually doesn't sound crazy in your head. Once those thoughts are out in the open, however, you'll realize just how ridiculous they sound.

II.
Wildlife, Creepy Crawlies, and Flora

Black bears: I used to be terrified of them, but not so much anymore. I've had enough encounters where I now understand that they will almost always run away from human contact. Except when they don't, as in the case of the dumpster bear at a campground in New York. It took a while to coax that one out of our campsite, and when he finally decided to lumber away, he chose a tree nearby to scratch his back, as if to say "I'll decide when I leave". I feel pretty comfortable during the day— I have bear mace at the ready— but night time really freaks me out. If you know anything about sleeping in the woods, you know that the sound of a squirrel or raccoon can sound like a four hundred pound bear. In those moments, I'm still fearful of them.

Grizzly and polar bears: Speaking of things that will never, ever happen, I will never camp in a place with either. One exception would be if I had a bear fence which is an electrified, light weight fencing you can put up around your tent— but this would only be acceptable for grizzlies in my mind. In fact, I'm pretty sure I will never go anywhere with polar bears, whether for a day trip or overnight. They actively stalk and view humans as prey. No thanks!

Relief!

Know where they're likely to be found.

Don't be an idiot: Don't antagonize wildlife. Make noise when going through dense areas. Don't approach them. Don't eat or cook near your tent. Change your clothes after cooking. Put your smellables in a bear box or canister. Use your head.

Know what to do (and not do): Don't go outside without knowing what do to if you encounter wildlife that doesn't want you as a houseguest. If you find yourself in an encounter, make plenty of noise and make yourself appear large. Stay close to your group. Never, EVER run. You cannot outrun a bear. Don't turn your back. A bear may bluff charge. If it attacks: Brown, stay down (face down, specifically, covering your neck with your pack on your back to protect your torso). Black, fight back. This rhyme surely has saved people from unfortunate bear encounters.

Arm yourself: Get some bear mace. It's the best $50 insurance policy you can buy. Studies have shown time and time again that bears hate it. Their eyesight is poor so they rely on their sense of smell— which is precisely what you're taking away from them when you use it. There are videos online of momma bears leaving their cubs to run up a tree when sprayed. Mace is much more effective than a firearm. It emits a spray far and wide, making good aim a non-issue (which is important, because at this point, you're probably shitting your pants in fear. There is no way you're going to aim well). Carry it everywhere— it saves bears and people. I suggest you purchase UDAP's brand. It was created by a man who was mauled by a bear. After surviving the experience, he wanted to make a better bear mace. Take a look at the photos taken of him after the attack. You'll trust him in a heartbeat. I'm certain he's making a good product.

Practice unholstering the canister before going out in the woods. Not all maces come with a holster (I now prefer to put it in the side of my pack), but wherever you decide to put it, practice taking it out. Make it muscle memory. On one hike, I went ahead of the group and after turning a corner found a black bear in the path. At that time, I had the mace in its holster. I couldn't get it out. It was like a glove. Even though I had the tools to defend myself, I would have been screwed if I really needed it. Practice!

Statistics: At the time of writing, in North America, there have only been sixty two fatal black bear attacks since 1900. Your chances of dying in a bear attack are ridiculously slim. Sure, there will be rogue bears out there, but if you follow the standards for not being an asshole, you're probably going to be fine.

Mountain lions: Even though I don't have to think about them in my native New Jersey, when I am out west they are at the forefront of my mind. As I'm walking through the woods I recount news stories— one of a couple taking a lovely stroll, only to find a mountain lion had been stalking them and jumped at one of their necks the first chance he got. I know that these things don't happen too often, but sometimes, you feel like you'll be the exception to the rule. Someone has to be. There have been times when I have insisted on turning around, feeling as though I was being watched. I always bring my bear mace and find a large stick to carry around. Even armed with bear mace and a stick, mountain lions are the reason I haven't camped out west yet.

Relief!

Know where they're likely to be found.

Know what to do (and not do): First and foremost, if you're with kids, pick them up. If you have a pet with you, leash them in. Make yourself appear as large as possible and stay close to your companions. Raise and wave your arms slowly. Make noise and/or speak loudly, firmly, and slowly. Always maintain eye contact. Do not make yourself appear like prey— never crouch down, turn you back, or make any sudden movements. Throw things at it and create distance slowly to allow the mountain lion to retreat. If you're attacked, fight back with everything you have. Be sure to protect your neck and throat.

Statistics: It's rare to see a mountain lion let alone be attacked by one.

Arm yourself: Carry around a large stick or bear mace. It can't hurt.

Snakes: They don't freak me out too much. What scares me is when Nick chides me on and claims he'll catch it, usually referring to a rattlesnake. He never does it, but I think he gets some sort of satisfaction out of making me squirm. For a while I carried around a snake bite kit, but later learned that they were bullshit.

Relief!

Know where they're likely to be found: Snakes especially like tall grass, piles of leaves, rocks (and crevices), and piles of wood. Research destination specific types you're likely to encounter.

Don't be an idiot: If you see a venomous snake, don't try to pick it up, trap it, or threaten it in any way.

Know what to do (and not do): If bitten, immediately call 911 or your park specific ranger number. Note any distinguishing features of the snake in order for medical personnel to identify it. Keep calm and still and lay with the bite below heart level. Wash with soap and water and cover. Don't wait for symptoms to appear before seeking medical attention. Do not fashion a tourniquet or attempt to extract the venom.

Statistics: According to the CDC, 7,000- 8,000 people are bitten by venomous snakes in the United States every year. About five of them die. Seek medical care and the odds will certainly be with you.

Venomous Spiders: Nick is the world's largest man child whenever he encounters a spider. They are my strong suit. Luckily, Jersey doesn't have many poisonous ones, so bite away.

Relief!

Know where they're likely to be found: Check your shoes before putting them on. If you're in an area where they're prevalent, shake out clothes before getting dressed. Before picking up firewood, inspect it. Know what destination specific types you're likely to encounter.

Know what to do (and not do): If bitten, look for distinguishing markings on the spider if it's still around. Wash the area with soap and water and ice it. Seek medical attention. Do not attempt to extract venom.

Bees: I don't know how, but I've never been stung by a bee. I'd like to note here that I don't have any known allergies. But because I've never been stung, I have no clue if I'm allergic. I've thought about getting an epi pen from the doctor just in case, but I fear he would give me a referral for a psychiatrist instead.

Relief!

Know what to do (and not do): If stung, remove the stinger. Wash with warm, soapy water and ice the affected area. If you're allergic, make sure you use your epi pen and head straight to the ER. If it's your first time being stung and you find you're having an allergic reaction, or are stung numerous times, head to the ER.

Ticks: Oh, boy. I've had some serious bad luck with these guys. I was sick for months. I initially realized that something was wrong when my knees started hurting (arthritis is typically a late stage symptom of lyme disease). The pain started in one knee and the other knee quickly followed suit. It had gotten so bad that I couldn't get myself on or off of the toilet— Nick would have to come in and help me. I was treated with a month long course of antibiotics and the pain subsided after about a week (though they've never been *quite* the same since). A couple of months later, I was starting to feel off again. I went back to the doctor and was tested for lyme disease again as well as other tick borne illnesses. The test came back positive for babesia— and I was one of less than one hundred confirmed cases in the U.S. at that time. Babesia can be pretty severe— it attacks your red blood cells and sometimes can deplete your bone marrow. I was treated with a hefty medication that is also used for malaria.

Relief!

Know where they're likely to be found: Be mindful of walking through tall grass where ticks like to congregate. Try to stay on the trail if possible. Some areas are especially known for their tick presence— if traveling through these areas take extra precautions.

Know what to do (and not do): Wear long, light colored pants if possible as it makes ticks easy to spot. Wear a hat or bandana to keep them out of your hair. Check your entire body with a flashlight when you get home— you have at least twenty four hours before lyme and other infections are transmittable.

Some people swear by permethrin— a spray that repels and kills ticks (and mosquitoes and mites). It is sprayed on your clothing and gear and lasts through numerous washings. I choose not to use it because it is extremely toxic to cats. We have a furry friend at home so we don't want to take any chances.

Bed Bugs: I will never underestimate their prevalence again. I would usually do a quick once over of our room, but I've started to perform a full scale investigation after we had gotten them in Colorado. It was horrendous. I have never seen Nick so defeated— he was ready to throw everything away, eat the cost of a new return flight and get the hell home. Although I broke down for a time myself, I decided that there was no way I was throwing away upwards of $700 of gear *plus* the cost of a new plane ticket *plus* a completely ruined vacation. I bucked up and made mental notes in my head on what to do first. It's like a "chicken or the egg" scenario. Cross contamination was a serious threat and there was no way I was bringing them home. $20 in quarters later, five loads of washing and drying, two new hotels, two new duffel bags, a new rental car, and we were on our way. We had a "fuck it" moment and ended up snowmobiling in Yellowstone. Though I never, ever want to experience bedbugs again, that was a decent payoff. I'm sure Nick would concur.

Relief!

Know what to do (and not do): Check reviews of hotels before booking. Don't bring your luggage in the room until you check everything using the flashlight on your phone: mattress and box springs (especially around the seams), dust ruffle, bed frame, headboard, pictures, end tables, furniture, and dressers. The signs include skins, carcasses, fecal spots, and blood spots. If you find anything, run!

Poison Oak, Ivy, Sumac: I have never gotten poison ivy. I can't imagine that after years spent tromping through the woods that I can get it. I'd like to think I'm immune to it— though it doesn't stop me from washing my hands incessantly before I touch my face or anything I'm going to eat. I make sure the valve on my water bladder doesn't brush foliage as I'm walking along the trail. Before we pack up the car, I even put a small piece of foil over it, just in case oils are on our packs or in the car. My biggest fear is having a pulmonary reaction (while rare, it isn't impossible).

Relief!

Know what to do (and not do): Never, ever, ever burn any type of poison as it can cause a dangerous pulmonary reaction. If you have a severe reaction or one that is on your face or genitals, or it comes with swelling, seek medical attention. Rinse the area of exposure with warm, soapy water. Wash all clothing and surfaces. Try not to scratch— an over the counter treatment can help.

I recently found a manufacturer that makes a pre and post poison wipe. It is said to lessen the effects if you don't have access to soap and water. I have yet to use it (I don't really need to) but the reviews are fantastic.

III.
Humans

As if I wasn't neurotic enough, Nick once made a comment about how I'm so concerned with wildlife, but what I should really be concerned with is people. Luckily, we've only had one instance that left me uncomfortable.

We were on a lightly used portion of the Appalachian Trail in New Jersey. We saw someone with a camp set up cliff side and, of course, Nick just had to talk to him. It became obvious quite quickly that this guy was mentally unstable. He claimed to be thru hiking the AT all alone (his gear cache said otherwise— this was a legitimate car camping set up— full size axe included) and that his wife had met him twenty miles back to pick up all of the guns he had initially packed.

Amongst a slew of other non believable things this guy claimed, our favorite was when he described fighting off a black bear with a knife in each hand. It got very, very weird. We were trying to continue on our way but he just wouldn't let the conversation end. We decided to just start walking and he still tried to continue the conversation. I was looking behind me for a good mile to make sure he wasn't following us.

Relief!

Know what to do (and not do): Use your head. Don't travel in dark, deserted alleys. Try to stay around populated areas. If I'm in an area that's seedy or if I don't want to be bothered by anyone (panhandlers or otherwise), I'll walk briskly with my husband and act as though we're having a passionate discussion so no one could get a word in edgewise. If I'm alone, I'll talk to someone on my phone with my pepper spray key ring in the other hand. Stay alert. If I'm especially sketched out by the area, I'll turn my engagement ring around with the diamond facing my palm. I don't carry a purse when traveling (and no, Mom, I won't be wearing a fanny pack). Same goes for the woods. Use your head!

Don't go alone: I'm probably going to take a lot of heat for this one, but it's just safer to travel (and especially hike) in numbers.

Arm yourself: A small can of pepper spray can't hurt.

Look for an out: If you start to get weirded out, look around for an escape route before it becomes a necessity.

"When forced to make a decision, most people will do the right thing": Spoken by the late Senator Merlino of New Jersey, it helps to remember this. Of course, there are people out there who wouldn't give you the time of day but there are far more people willing to help you. You're never alone on the road or trail and people all over are largely good hearted. Through our Couch Surfing experiences and staying with friends of relatives, we found that most people love to be hospitable. We were taken in, made comfortable, and shared meals— which I consider to be one of the most intimate acts with a stranger. It's so base, so necessary to our existence, and so humbling to break bread with others.

IV.
The Weather

Nothing quite gets me down as much. I literally have no control over it, though I can try to not place myself in bad situations. Sometimes, however, weather just *happens*.

Thunderstorms: I love them from the comfort of my own home. If you've ever been in the woods in one, you'll know it isn't quite as romantic and cozy. I have never heard thunder rumbling so loud as when I've been caught in it outdoors. All of my childhood warnings come into my head— get inside, it isn't safe to be outdoors. Thunder makes me jump, but lightening is the real danger. I get it— as long as I'm not in a field or on an exposed rock face I'm probably going to be okay. Once, when caught in a lightning storm, I proceeded to run as fast as I could— as if I could outrun a lightning strike. That's surely the cave woman in me coming out.

Tornadoes: Never been in one, never seen one from a distance, and don't intend to. I pretty much avoid the middle of the country like the plague during the shoulder seasons. To see news footage of its destruction, namely houses and cars literally thrown around, is enough for me.

Flash floods: I have such a strong desire to see the slot canyons in Utah and Arizona. When we visited Arches National Park, I had a surprising connection to the land— the red rocks and contours are breathtaking. Knowing that they are literally changing by the day is a special treat. What's holding me back ever so slightly is watching too many internet videos of people being caught in a deluge of murky, muddy water running like rapids through the canyons.

Hurricanes: These are pretty easy to avoid if you bother looking at the news at all. Before Hurricane Irene, I was checking radar maps, ready to get Nick, his dad, and the cat all packed up and into Pennsylvania where she wouldn't touch. During Hurricane Sandy, Nick and I were on our honeymoon in California. I was so, so happy. It's bad enough being somewhere you're comfortable; traveling during one of these must be hell.

Earthquakes: I've been in two. The first was in Hawai'i in 2006, and that was a pretty big one with several large aftershocks. What really scared me about it was that I was working a block from the beach at the time. No one could call out on their cell phones; no one seemed to know if there was a tsunami warning in place. The second was in Jersey (crazy, right?!) and that was pretty small. Not so bad at home, but on the road I'd imagine that it's pretty scary.

You don't always know the correct course of action. To mitigate that problem, a hotel we stayed at in Mill Valley, California, had laminated instructions on the dresser outlining what to do in the event of an earthquake. Even furniture was bolted to the walls. They can happen without warning anywhere, but what freaks me out is that in a place like California, you're literally just waiting for the next one. I think about it when we're driving over bridges and imagine the whole thing falling into the bay. It's only a matter of time until the next one comes.

Relief!

Don't get summit fever: You've heard the stories—people want to get to their destination even though storm clouds are looming. This is how people die. Don't do it, just don't. We had to turn around (rather than camp) on the Kalalau Trail in Kaua'i because of rain and the risk of flash flooding. Who knows what would have happened had we stayed? In 1985, five hikers were climbing Half Dome in Yosemite National Park. They ignored signs and warnings of a thunderstorm, and only three made it out alive. This goes for every weather scenario possible— if you are being warned by mother nature— heed that warning and get back to safety. It doesn't matter how much vacation time or money was wasted. Go back.

Check the weather: Before you head out, just check it. It might save you a lot of trouble or your life. Just rain can damage trails and make them more dangerous than they already are. If the weather is questionable and you decide to depart anyway, check it during your hike if you can.

Know what to do (and not do): There are about a million different scenarios we could run through here, and each is typically destination specific. If you're going to an area known for weather, or will be there during certain times of the year, know what to expect!

Know what to do if you get caught outdoors in a thunderstorm. Know what to do if you get caught outdoors in a thunderstorm <u>above tree line.</u> Know CPR just in case. Have the ranger and emergency numbers for the area. Have maps (and study them beforehand) to educate yourself on your surroundings. Whenever we hike above tree line, I see where the quickest route down to the forest begins. You never know.

Sun exposure: It can be more dangerous than you might think. On a trip to Yosemite, I was out too long in the sun (at altitude) without proper protection for a couple of days. After the weekend concluded, I wasn't feeling well. We were driving to our next destination and I felt sick to my stomach. I tried to eat and I couldn't. I was dizzy and having trouble concentrating. I felt like I was drunk and hadn't had a sip. We decided to go to the emergency room. I have an angioma in my brain, that, while unlikely, can bleed (it has in the past) so we didn't want to take any chances. I was shocked when the doctor told me I had sun poisoning. It hadn't even occurred to me that could be a possibility. After about two hours and two bags of saline, I was good to go.

Relief!

Protect yourself: Use sunscreen, wear hats, drink plenty of water, and try to limit skin exposure.

Altitude: It is overlooked a lot of the time. Here in Jersey, we're at sea level— the air is more oxygenated and it's easier to breathe. At high altitudes, a hike you could blow through at sea level can feel like a marathon. Nick and I were hiking at the flatirons in Boulder, Colorado one winter. We initially were only going to walk up to them and take photographs, so we only brought a small amount of water. Our curiosity got the better of us— we saw a trail marker showing the way to an arch (the only naturally occurring one in the state!) so we decided to continue on as it wasn't that far. No food, no more water to speak of, and not being used to the altitude, we were in for a shitty hike. On the way back down, I started feeling quite woozy and wasn't sure if I would make it. Be sure to have plenty to eat and drink!

Relief!

Know what to do (and not do): Take frequent breaks and eat and drink more than you think you need. If you're feeling extra shitty, make your way down. The only real cure for altitude sickness is to go down.

Winter: Whether it be frozen drinking water, getting hurt and stuck overnight in the elements, avalanches, or hypothermia, winter can be a scary time of year to be outdoors. To make matters worse, there are less people out and about so if you do run into trouble you may not have help. If you do need help, it will take much longer for rescuers to slog through snow and ice to reach you.

Relief!

Use your resources: Call the ranger station on the days leading up to (and the day of) your trip. They'll be able to give you precise weather and trail reports.

Have the proper gear: Don't venture out without winter specific items (snowshoes, micro spikes, crampons, ice axe, wind breaker, sunglasses, layers, and on and on). It may be advantageous to ask the ranger station what gear is recommended for your trail of choice. Be aware though, certain trails require you to at least carry snowshoes, even if they aren't needed. We were stopped by a ranger once but luckily we had them lashed to our packs. If we didn't have them we would have been ticketed.

Try it out first: If you're unfamiliar with the area or terrain, something Nick and I like to do is walk about a half hour to an hour of the trail the day before we plan on taking the hike. It's easier to see what you're in for and you can speak with people who pass you on their way down to get some intel.

Beware of the water bladder: If you use a bladder for your water, think about reconsidering. The lines have a tendency to freeze in the winter, and while there are products on the market meant to curtail this, the best thing you can do is use plastic Nalgene-esque bottles with an old wool sock on the outside as a sleeve. If it's really, really cold, you can place a hand warmer between the sock and the bottle.

Be prepared: Always be prepared to spend the night outdoors. You might be able to wing it in the summer, but winter weather might preclude this as an option. Have plenty of extra clothing, a shelter, and a lot of extra food and water. You become more dehydrated in the cold which can lead to hypothermia.

Know hypothermia prevention: Wear wool or other wicking layers (cotton kills!). The key is to stay warm and dry. If you start to sweat, stop to remove layers. Drink and eat more than you think you need to and take frequent breaks.

Know the signs of hypothermia: When cold, you'll shiver. As hypothermia sets in, you'll stop shivering. You'll become clumsy and uncoordinated. Your speech may be slurred or you might be prone to mumbling. You'll be drowsy and it will be difficult for you to make good decisions.

Know what to do in the event of hypothermia: If your hiking partner is unconscious, seek medical attention immediately. Afterwards, move your partner to a shelter very carefully. Remove wet clothes and replace them with dry ones. If they're able to hold a cup, give them something warm to drink (preferably something sugary). If your partner is able to, have them move around a little to generate heat; if they are unable, place them in a sleeping bag, making sure to insulate the floor beneath and to trap air above it. Do not put them in hot water as this can cause shock.

Know your area: If you're in an area prone to avalanches, look for updates on avalanche reports and carry a beacon. Brush up on your self-arrest skills. Remember, you're at the whim of the weather. If the forecast is gnarly, don't go.

Don't be scared: I was pretty frightened before our first major winter hike, but we did certain things that helped me feel more comfortable. We read a bunch of trip reports, chose a good trail for a first time winter hike, called the ranger station to inquire about the trail and weather, hiked a bit of the trail the day before, and went hiking with another experienced partner. I can say, hands down, that hike was the best hike I've ever taken. The quietness is insane— there is literally no one around. The trail takes on a completely different feel with everything blanketed in white. Luckily, the trail was packed well and few spots were icy— making what would be a moderate summer hike turn into a gradual slope to the summit. The cold was the perfect complement to the day and made me feel vibrant and full of life.

V.
Night

I know I sound like a child here, but the dark scares me. Let me rephrase that— the dark scares me when I'm in a tent. I feel as though all of my senses have been stripped away from me. I can only imagine what is lurking behind those thin nylon walls.

I have to wear glasses when driving at night because my vision is terrible once the sun goes down. When we climb into our tent, I tell Nick I'm not tired yet and I attempt to get away with leaving the light on. He always calls my bluff and promptly turns it off.

I would wear earplugs if I didn't think it was a safety issue. I often wake Nick up in the middle of the night, asking him what this sound or that sound was. He's started making it a point when we arrive at our campsite to tell me to take a look around. He points out that they are the same woods, the only difference is that it will be dark later.

As a throwback to my childhood days, I'm still convinced that everything bad happens at night. I spent too many nights sleeping on my parents' bedroom floor as a child, terrified of the boogeyman (and I still kind of am).

And, while we're at it, overnight backpacking trips are pretty difficult for me. I have a hard enough time car camping:

Many of our relatives lived in the Pine Barrens of New Jersey when I was young (and many still do). Those woods were incredibly mysterious and frightening to me. I hated staying at my Aunt Carol's (for this reason only— love Aunt Carol!). Even in a great big house, the woods felt like they were closing in on me. Instead of hearing cars and people, all I heard were trees blowing in the wind and crickets chirping.

I'd lie in bed and listen, imagining all of the terrifying things out there under the cover of brush and darkness. Plus, the Jersey Devil was said to wander the Pine Barrens. I could barely look out the window at night.

My first and only camping experience as a child was when I was twelve years old and traveling with my Aunt Joanne, Uncle Steven and my two cousins, Kate and Hannah. Our destination happened to be the Catskill Mountains in New York State. After a three hour drive, we pulled up to our reserved campsite which was within striking distance of a literal pig pen. Yes, an actual pen with pigs in it and all of the smells that come with them— right next to our sleeping quarters. It was almost cartoonish in its absurdity. Aunt Joanne was livid, demanding her money be returned to her, while the indifference of the clerk was insufferable. She didn't seem to understand why someone would have a problem with a few pigs.

Discouraged, we drove around for what seemed like an eternity (before the dawn of smart phones and reviews on lodging and services) to find another campground. We found one that seemed fitting— there were many families there, a pool to relax in, and plenty of woods to explore. We partook in the usual camping activities— telling stories, roasting marshmallows, and playing cards. Everything was going great until night fell.

We had an enormous tent with a porch area in the front to accommodate the five of us. In the middle of the night, I woke up in a sweat, swearing to myself and my bleary eyed aunt that someone (or something) was rummaging around in our porch area. I could hear rustling and see shadows moving across the tent walls. There were rowdy campers around (clearly drunk) and all of the excitement was making me nervous.

Rather than get out of bed to look and assuage my fears, my aunt, being a good motherly figure, refused. She asserted that there was nothing to be afraid of. As an adult, I realize that she was trying to give me the tools to calm myself, to internally find the confidence to know that I was okay. As a twelve year old in a strange place, however, I just wasn't getting it. I proceeded to cry and chastise myself for agreeing to this horrible trip in the first place. I woke my aunt up again, whose solution this time was to pray together. As someone who never took comfort in this sort of thing, it only served to make my anxiety worse. I internalized my fear just so I wouldn't have to pray with Aunt Joanne any longer.

I finally fell asleep and awoke the next morning to find the woods exactly as they had been the day before. It seemed to me that they changed as night fell and shifted back into their normal form again before the dawn. I couldn't wait to get home and vowed that I would never go camping again.

Nonetheless, Nick and I have been on numerous camping trips together. Nine out of every ten trips I wake up in our tent, soaked in sweat, heart racing so fast that I can no longer hear the sounds outside that caused the anxiety, and bear mace at the ready. Every time I read of a camper attacked in their tent by a bear only serves to fuel this crazy fire. I know that logically, I'm way safer sleeping out in the woods than I am even at home, but all logic goes out the window in the middle of the night. Fallacies are abundant when I'm in a panic— I'm the .000001%. I'm the one who will experience a horrible mishap.

I once saw a psychologist to talk about this fear,

and comically, the receptionist asked what I'd be doing that weekend. I told her I was going camping and she asked if I had heard the news story about the local guy who went camping with his family and was struck by an errant tree branch. He died right next to his wife and kids. It just didn't seem like camping was in the cards for me— the universe (and complete strangers) were telling me to stay inside at night. I thought the more I camped the easier it would become. In my head, it only increased the chances that something awful would happen. You won't believe it— but this is only car camping! The car is right there and the keys are at the ready if we need to make a quick retreat. I usually fall asleep with them right beside me, the car positioned at a straight shot from the tent door if possible.

As I've demonstrated, Nick has an inexhaustible thirst for adventure. While it may be easy to brush off crazy requests to go wing suit flying, climb Everest, or BASE jump, it doesn't make sense for me to dismiss his desire to go on multiday hiking trips. I desperately want to go— not only for him— but for me as well. I finally gave in, not to a multiday trip, but to a wilderness camping experience. We were going to Round Valley Reservoir in Lebanon, New Jersey. We would canoe to our campsite with no access to the outside world other than by boat or foot.

The trip didn't start off well to begin with. We were supposed to leave on a Friday to meet Nick's brother John and his girlfriend Shadis, who were already at the site. We needed paddles and life jackets and thinking we could find them easily we waited until Thursday night to purchase them. After picking up some groceries, we went to a sporting goods store and that was a bust. We called up several other big box stores, which were also no gos. Giving up for the night, we resumed the search the following morning. It took us from early morning until late afternoon to find suitable paddles and life jackets. We resolved to leave on Saturday morning— just in time for a mere 30% chance of thunderstorms on the radar for that night. I looked on the park's website and there was not a structure to be found to take refuge in. Not wanting to disappoint Nick (or myself), I ignored the gnawing feeling inside that something awful would happen. I was ignoring mother nature's warning to stay away, which I was certain would not end well for me.

We strapped our canoe on the roof of our car and hit the road for the hour drive. For that hour, we listened to what sounded like a massive swarm of bees. Somehow, the wind catches just right on the ratchet straps and is the worst sound on earth above forty miles per hour. If anyone has an experience with this, you know that it is akin to torture. Flustered (yet relieved!), we approached the boat launch (which took forever to locate) and laid our canoe out on the water for the voyage. We were both frustrated as we paddled— the reservoir was relatively calm but we were still pushing against the wind. Being an inexperienced paddler, I was offering very little help.

After a couple of hours, we reached our site and got to work setting up camp. Everything seemed to be going well. Nick's friend Mike and his dog even joined us for the weekend. We relaxed on the shore and Nick taught me (albeit unsuccessfully) how to skip rocks. We took our vessels out for a late afternoon paddle and it was just the rest and relaxation we needed after the hectic scrambling to make the trip happen.

Later on, Nick and the guys wanted to take a night paddle, but Shadis and I were adamant— the thunderstorms were swiftly approaching and there was no way they were going. We heard some fireworks and went to the shore where we were met with a wonderful show from a nearby town. In the midst of this, we heard what sounded like a freight train heading straight for us, followed by an ear piercing wind siren positioned on the shore to let boaters know when to get off of the water. We started running to our site. The rain started and the 30% chance of thunderstorms was not in our favor. The sky rumbled and lit up. Of course, with only a 30% chance of storms, it would storm. I should have known better.

During all of the excitement, I proceeded to feel incredibly ill (I probably had a bit of motion sickness from the long paddle) and threw everything I had eaten up. We were huddled under tarps and I was shaking uncontrollably. I was definitely having a panic attack— nausea, tight chest, the sensation that I couldn't breathe— and there was literally no way out. I was terrified that I was going to get struck by lightning, or a tree would fall on us, or that my heart would just stop. I couldn't just hop in the canoe— that was practically a death wish. Many people have drowned in the reservoir when the weather turns as it often does. There was no way I could hike out— I could barely breathe and my nausea precluded this as an option.

I had nothing to do but tell myself what I often do when I get panicky. People do this all of the time and nothing ever happens. I pretended that I was someone else, someone confident and trusting of the natural order of things to know that everything would be okay.

The rain and thunderstorms finally stopped but the wind was still whipping when we retreated into our tents for the night. I chuckled at myself and my incessant worrying when I saw Mike climb into his hammock with his dog. Two minutes later his snoring began. I was in a tent and was worried about the wind while Mike was welcoming it, inviting it to sway him to sleep.

I laid in the tent, eyes wide open, listening to the wind. I heard Nick grinding his teeth and I knew he had fallen asleep. I was alone in my consciousness and my mind started to wander again. The tent was shaking and I was certain we were just going to be thrown up into the sky and blown away. As dawn approached, I eased into a fitful nap as I always do. I feel as though an hour before dawn I can finally relax. The sun would be shining soon and there would be nothing to fear.

The next day we had a leisurely paddle out, hugging the shoreline, playing bumper boats. We returned to the launch and while we were ratchet strapping our vessels to our roofs, Nick and I grumbled about our impending loud drive home. John handed us four lengths of rope and we tied them onto the straps to see if that would dampen the noise. We had such a blissfully quiet drive home. We had an amazing breakfast at a local diner where a lone man was covering Neil Young songs in the foyer— just him and his guitar. The excursion came in like a lion and out like a lamb.

Though no one was in any immediate danger (even though it seemed that way to me at the time), one of my worst case scenarios came to life. I felt sick, but I ended up being okay. There were thunderstorms, but no one was struck by lightning. There was wind, but no one was crushed by a tree. We were alone out there and that was perfectly fine. Nothing happened. This was several years ago, and while opportunities have presented themselves, I haven't quite mustered up the guts to get back out there— until May of 2014, when Nick and I choose our first real backpacking excursion.

I had lived in Hawai'i for many years and Nick had never visited. As soon as we were able, we booked our trip. Upon researching possible destinations and hikes, Nick set his hooks into the Kalalau Trail. It's a life list hike— you're rewarded with amazing views and the ocean by your side. The trail climbs eleven miles in and out of valleys, eventually ending at an inaccessible (to most) beach.

I tore through our gear closet, searching for everything we would need to complete the hike. I added to the gear pile for months before our trip, purchasing what was needed for the trek. I thought of every contingency: I read a ton of trip reports, looked at countless maps, and knew where we could find water. I knew the dangers of the trail: no cell phone service, flash flooding, and steep drop offs (there is even a portion of the trail called "crawler's ledge"). I went as far as purchasing a personal locator beacon for emergencies (this trip was the impetus for that wish list purchase!). I mailed food and camping gear to our accommodations so we didn't have to travel with everything. I was hesitant, but I chalked it up to inexperience. I was certain I had thought of everything.

Two weeks before our departure, I realized that we didn't have permits. We were so busy preparing for the rest of the trip that we overlooked it. This is a popular trail with limited permits available, so I knew we might not be successful. Our inter-island flights were already booked so we only had a specific window of time in which we could hike. We ended up changing our inter-island flights to accommodate permit availability. Our first mistake was forgetting the permits and our second mistake quickly followed— the only permits that were available had us hiking a mere day after an eleven hour flight.

We made it to Kauai without a problem. We were having difficulty adjusting to the six hour time difference and were exhausted from traveling so we didn't set out for the trailhead until about noon. There is a campsite, Hanakoa, about six miles in. We figured we'd make it there before nightfall without issue and hike the rest of the way the following day. Two nights at Kalalau Beach still sounded amazing.

We reached the trailhead, our backs heavy with roughly thirty pounds each. About a quarter of a mile in, as promised, there were already spectacular views. The beach was to the right, the great Pacific Ocean in front, and the valleys we'd be required to traverse lay out before us. To say we were in awe would be an understatement.

While reading about the trail, people complained about the humidity again and again. I thought hikers were exaggerating, but, unfortunately, they weren't. The humidity was horrendous and sucked the energy right out of me. The times of shade were few and far between. I was hot and uncomfortable and knew the day would be long and arduous.

The contrast between the red soil of the trail, the lush green valleys, and the deep blue ocean was magnificent. The first two miles of the trail were steep, only leveling out occasionally to give your calves a break. Along the trail there were numerous helicopter landing sites, a reminder of how dangerous it can be and how strict the state is about permits. We've heard many stories of rangers being brought onto the trail via helicopter to give out tickets. Our first stream crossing was a blessing and I took a much needed break to cool off.

We passed many people on the trail, but once we hit Hanakāpī'ai Beach at mile two it was apparent how popular the path was. It was here that I started getting cold feet about the whole thing. I had never been out on an overnight before, I was run ragged from all of the traveling, and I wasn't feeling confident. Nick and I had a bit of a spat as we continued on the trail—I wanted to turn back and he wanted to continue. The trail was a lot more challenging than I had imagined, and something just didn't feel right. I felt as though I shouldn't be there. The discussion continued as we started following a stream bed. I had reserved to suck it up and continue on. As I'm telling myself "you've got this", I slipped and twisted my ankle.

I could walk on it, but it was painful. At this point, we were roughly four miles in and had another two to go until we reached the campsite. We would continue on— the hardest part of the trail was behind us, we had already passed the halfway point, and if we turned around we'd be hiking in the dark. We figured if my ankle was bad in the morning we could flag down a passing boat (the Nāpali coastline is very popular for sightseeing) and hitch a ride out. It was slow going, but we were making progress.

Nick started breaking down. He was upset with himself for not listening to me and turning around when I asked. As my husband, of course, he felt the responsibility of getting me safely to our destination and he was overwhelmed. He was shutting down and becoming agitated. We crossed streams numerous times, not stopping to collect or thoughts or have a bite to eat. We were feeling vulnerable in a strange place five thousand miles away from home. We *had* to make it to the campsite before dark.

We then walked up to a three hundred foot waterfall. There was no longer a discernible trail. This is the stuff that movies are made of— here we are, dwarfed by this massive waterfall, any thoughts or vocalizations were drowned out by the sound of water gushing from its top. Nick frantically ran around looking for the trail, but I stayed put. It was obvious to me that there was no trail. We were at a dead end. Over and over I told Nick there was no trail— partly to have him stop wasting time, partly to allow myself to come to terms with what was happening. Right on cue, it started raining. There was nowhere to camp. The bulk of the trail was stream (the area is notorious for flash floods) and cliff side. There was no way I was camping on the beach we passed— it didn't seem safe to me. It was 5:30 in the evening, there was nowhere to camp, and we were (to put it lightly) screwed.

We saw a group of three people our age and Nick asked them where the Kalalau Trail was. One pointed behind us and responded "a few miles that way". I couldn't believe it— after all of the research I had done, all of the maps I had studied— we missed the trail junction. In the midst of our disagreement, we didn't realize we weren't supposed to be following a stream, we were supposed to be cliff side. It never occurred to us that when hikers we passed said "you're almost at the falls!" that we were on the wrong trail. I thought *they* were confused.

At this point we made the worst mistake possible— we started panicking. Nick never panics and I knew we were in over our heads. I'm not sure I've ever been so frightened— I knew we'd be hiking in the dark on the most gnarly part of the trail. The group we had met was long gone and we were on our own. In my panic, I started making mistakes. Stream crossings were no longer calculated but increasingly sloppy. I fell many times, taking blows to my shins and countless baths I hadn't intended on taking. At one crossing, I couldn't move. I was paralyzed with fear. Nick was pleading with me to get up and I snapped out of it, all the while begging him to call ahead to the group and ask them to wait for us. Within a few moments, Nick fell. I instinctually screamed. If Nick couldn't handle this, how on earth could I? Our fellow trail companions didn't respond to the blood curdling scream I had let out. It felt as though we were truly alone.

Eventually, we ended up catching up to the group at another stream crossing. I was so relieved and decided that we would follow them the whole way back. We told them our situation and they waited for us at every turn. They assisted Nick in getting me over numerous stream crossings, stopping my fall more than once.

We soon learned their names— Casey, who seemed to have lived a thousand different lives and bore an uncanny resemblance in demeanor to Nick's cousin Drew; Yukiah, a woman from South Africa; and Olivier, a man from the Alps. When Nick and I realized that we didn't have to do this on our own, our nerves were instantly soothed. The duty was now shared— it was everyone's responsibility to look out for the group's safety. Casey noticed my fear and said something that really helped: in situations like these, people panic but fail to realize that nothing has changed. Only the goal and your perception has changed. I should mention here that Casey was wearing a Jurassic Park tee shirt and I instantly liked him. They all lived in Kilauea, literally on the same street as our bed and breakfast. They'd hiked the trail numerous times so we felt as though we were in good hands. We spoke on so many topics, some incredibly personal, and definitely connected with the group on a level we never thought was possible on the trail. Who knows where the fear would have led us if we hadn't met them. We recognize that we might not have such a benign story to tell.

When we reached the beach, Nick tried to persuade me to set up camp, gently asking if we could hike the rest of the way the next day. There was no way— I felt every inch of my being screaming to get the hell out of there. He would have continued but I didn't have it in me. I felt as though it just wasn't meant to be and we were lucky to have even made it to this point unscathed.

The group began searching for another member of their party. As it turns out, we passed a man on our way in (with him on his way out) matching his description. We pressed on and found Scott (who we would later call the mad scientist because at one time he worked for NASA) and continued together.

Night fell and we pulled out our headlamps. They had one between the four of them and Nick and I each had our own. We divvied them up and walked single file in the dark. Yukiah and I pressed ahead and led the group. We were both done. Every time we saw a trail marker we rejoiced. We walked for over an hour in the dark until we finally emerged from the woods. I wanted to kiss the ground— we made it out!

We were invited to their place for dinner and drinks, but we were spent. We needed food immediately and a shower was long overdue. We went our separate ways and traveled back to the bed and breakfast. We moseyed into the common area, telling our B & B companions of our tale. At the end of the day, we had ended up hiking about nine and a half miles with full packs. The entire trail was eleven. I know the mistakes we made and I trust we won't be making them again. Most importantly, though, I learned of the kindness of strangers.

Relief!

Don't be scared: Don't be a baby. You're surrounded by the same woods that were bathed in light, it's just pitch black. There are no monsters under the bed, there's no sasquatch, there's not really all that much to fear. You know you're prepared and that's the best you can do. Get some sleep and you might be less neurotic. You're almost always safer sleeping outside than you are at home.

VI.
On Being a Woman, Physically and Mentally

Nick's mantras when working out in preparation for hikes (adopted from the bodybuilders Ronnie Coleman and CT Fletcher) are:

"Ain't nothing but a peanut"

"Lightweight"

"It's still your fucking set"

You'd think there was a world class personal trainer in our bedroom. He's extremely good at being his own cheerleader, and while working out, he'll try to "motivate" me. In actuality, it's heckling. He's like that guy at the comedy shows that loves to mess with the comedian. Nick and I are roughly the same size, but of course, he's a man, and with that comes heavier weights. He'll comment on my lack of weight, tell me I'm a wimp (I'm using a nice term here), and tell me to just get it done. This is an extreme example of his attempts to treat me as an equal, but it's the perfect way to describe how our dynamic can be. This approach and attitude spills over into many aspects of our lives— the most notable of which is in hiking and outdoor sports. It is sometimes taxing to get the men in your life to understand that being an outdoorswoman can be difficult.

Without Nick, I can say for certain that I wouldn't have done the things I've done. He's helped me realize that I am almost always as capable as the next guy. I'm all for equality. There are things, however, that are just *different* for a woman. Not necessarily better or worse, just different. Hiking and being outdoors presents a unique set of circumstances for the ladies.

Bathroom breaks: Any woman can tell you the day she finally learned to pee in the woods without peeing on herself was an amazing victory. Even when you master it, you'll still pee on yourself occasionally. Sometimes it can't be helped.

It's tough to budget how much toilet paper we'll need on a hike. Some women are okay with leaves but I just don't trust my knowledge of poisonous plants.

Every single time we need to use the bathroom it's a huge ordeal. First, you have to find a spot that's well hidden from the trail, especially if it's a popular one. Then you have to find a suitable tree to lean on in an area that slopes downward. Personally, I like to make sure there aren't any rocks or briars underneath me in case I fall. There have been times where I ventured so far off of the trail to find a suitable spot that I had a tough time finding the trail again. Pack comes off, pants come down. If it's winter it's akin to torture.

Relief!

Tell your partner: Tell your hiking partner that you'll be making frequent stops and that it might take a while. I sometimes ask Nick to keep an eye out for a good spot if he sees one. If we come across one, I'll try to pee whether I need to go or not. Also, bring more toilet paper than you think you'll need. Always make sure you have an extra ziplock bag for used toilet paper- carry in, carry out!

Lady troubles: It just sucks. Having to figure out how many feminine products you'll need to last you is irksome. Having cramps, headaches, and generally feeling weak does not make for a good hike. It adds a rather annoying aspect to the already arduous task of peeing in the woods.

Relief!

Medicate: Take an anti-inflammatory to curb any symptoms. I like to take ZMA (a mix of zinc, magnesium, and b vitamins) for sports recovery and that really, really seems to help with my cramps once I do get my period. Also, try to eat foods high in iron the day prior— a good, old fashioned burger or cream of wheat is best.

Avoidance: If I can help it, I try to plan trips or hikes around my period.

Pack and weight: Our bodies are so vastly different that no amount of straps or adjustments can fix an ill fitting pack. You may think you've found the one, but after hours on the trail, you realize that the chest strap could be a little higher or the hip strap could be a little lower. Mere centimeters can make a difference. Thankfully, after a ton of research and trying on, I finally found my pack. Nick, however, was able to buy the first one he wanted and he loves it.

Most of us can't carry as much pack weight as men comfortably, especially if our packs don't fit properly in the first place. It makes me feel a bit bad that Nick has to carry more than I do.

Relief!

Take your time: Don't rush finding a pack. It will probably take longer than you think it will. Most major outdoor companies will take your measurements and try to find you the best packs based on your size. Try to purchase it from a company that allows returns... there's nothing worse than spending several hundred dollars to find out that after a couple of hikes (and countless adjustments) that it just doesn't work for you.

Hair: For the ladies with longer hair, this can become really bothersome. I find myself stopping more often to retie my hair or get it out of my face than I do for a break. If the hair tie is too tight you'll develop a headache; too loose and it'll just fall out. No hair tie and you're in for an uncomfortable trip. There is nothing worse than grimy, sweaty hair stuck to your face and back.

Relief!

Always carry extras: Always have extra hair ties, they can always be used for other things. Try a headband or bandanna if you want to change things up.

Sweat: I've ruined many a bra on the trail. The sweat makes the elastic wear out quickly, and the subsequent washings double the damage.

I also prefer to wear semi-form fitting hiking pants for tick prevention. I find that my range of motion is a bit better for scrambling but worse for sweating. When we stop to use the bathroom, we're also drying out.

On a hike in the Adirondacks, though it was a blissfully cool autumn day, I was sweating like a pig. I had my period at the time, and I decided to wear a pad because I wouldn't want to stop often enough to change a tampon. Very long story short, by the time I got home, I had what my gynecologist believed to be poison ivy. He prescribed me oral steroids and a topical cream. Three days passed and it was getting worse. I went to a dermatologist and she informed me that I had a staph infection. The sweat, couple with having shaved recently, coupled with showering in lake water made me a miserable mess for about two weeks.

Relief!

Change your gear: Try to find quick drying, wicking hiking pants. Better yet, try a skort and check your legs for ticks when your hike is over. Use only one bra specifically for sweaty activities or better yet, grab a sports bra.

Don't be dumb: Don't make the same mistake I did. If it sounds like a bad idea, it probably is.

Motherly instinct: I know that I can't speak for all women, but I believe that most of us want to nurture. I find myself acting like a mom on the trail— making sure no one is doing anything dangerous, making sure everyone is fueled and hydrated, making sure I've seen everyone in our group frequently, and running over a million worse case scenarios in my head. It's exhausting but built in and there is nothing any of us can do about it.

Knowing that if anything major happens, we may not be able to help an ailing hiking partner the same way a man can is troubling. We'd need a serious (and long lasting) dose of adrenaline to make it work.

There are going to be some things that we just can't do. That's a tough pill to swallow. When I approach anything that requires a high level of upper body strength, I'm crying on the inside. I can't always depend on my upper body strength no matter how many presses or rows I do. I often try to find an easier approach. Work smarter, not harder, right?

Relief!

Know your limits: Know that there is only so much you can do…but be prepared to help with what you can. Brains are sometimes more useful than brawn.

VII.
Odds and Ends

Waterways: There are literally countless ways to get in trouble on the water, whether you're a strong swimmer or not.

<u>Relief!</u>

The obvious: Wear life jackets, have important first aid and gear in waterproof, floating bags, and carry an air horn.

The not so obvious: Aside from the obvious obstacles like currents, riptides, and surf, be wary of lesser-known, destination specific threats— such as wana (sea urchin spines) and leptospirosis (a nasty water-borne disease that can kill), just to name a few. Nick had a piece of wana stuck in his foot for weeks— they're nearly impossible to remove, are super painful, and can become infected.

Planes, trains, and automobiles: I used to fly back and forth from Honolulu to Newark by myself at least twice a year. Flying never bothered me. I'd always been a little anxious before takeoff, but I think that was excitement more than anything else. These days, I'm a bit more nervous. I try to push it out of my mind in the weeks prior. It never fails though— the day of, I'm pretty bad. The anxiety hits its climax when I am sitting in the airplane, seat belt fastened, and we're taxing. I'm thinking to myself "this is your last chance to get off!". I play a scene in my head wherein I scream to get off of the plane and I run to safety. I've never done it. Once we're in the air, I'm pretty good. I just decide to give in because I don't really have any other choice.

I don't mind trains. In fact, I really like them. I just felt the need to include them for the sake of lyricism.

Car drives are tough for me, but less so than airplanes. At least there is the illusion of control. I can get out, stretch my legs, and go to the bathroom (without waiting for the seat belt sign to turn off). Not too shabby to me.

Relief!

People do this for a living (by choice!): When I start to get nervous on flights, I think about the stewardesses— they're just working through their shifts and running out the clock, just like we do on the ground. This is a perfectly normal day for them. Once, on Interstate 80 in Wyoming (a very desolate stretch of highway), the only thing that kept me from losing my mind was thinking about the truck drivers passing us. They do this every single day.

Know that the pilots and fellow drivers want to be safe: Mostly everyone wants to arrive at their destination safely. Sometimes it doesn't happen, but it makes me feel better to realize it. Those pilots have a family at home that they'd like to see. We're all human. Most of us fear death and the unknown. It's the way it should be— we're meant to be on this earth as long as possible to procreate. It's healthy on some level to fear death and scary shit. And that's what keeps us safe most of the time.

In view of a really bad year in air travel, it helps to remember that those are the exceptions, not the rule.

VIII.
Fear Itself

Being far from help/home: Medical emergencies are always in the back of my mind. Before I go anywhere, I find out how close the nearest hospital is. While I'm certainly looking out for number one, I'm more concerned for the people I'm with. Although I'm not a mother yet, I definitely feel that nurturing instinct kicking in already. I purchased the personal locator beacon precisely for this reason. If we can't make calls out, at least we can activate a search party. I'm not fearful of this when I'm home, just in places I'm unfamiliar with.

Relief!

People are the same everywhere: Most people are good, some are bad. I can guarantee, however, that if you were in trouble someone out there would help you. The reason we were able to create such a vast, populous society is because we looked out for one another.

Get a personal locator beacon: Even if you're just traveling in the middle of nowhere, if you're in serious trouble, someone will find you. It's a wonderful thing.

Be self reliant: Take a wilderness survival course and/or a backcountry first aid course. You can go the free route (many outdoor retailers and hiking groups offer them) and take several different classes, such as orienteering, shelter building, or general first aid to build up a knowledge base. Cheap courses are also available through local outdoor groups and they are typically more in depth. Wilderness first aid courses are especially intriguing— they offer CPR, backcountry first aid, and anaphylaxis instruction all in one place.

Is there an outdoor skill that you lack? You'd be surprised— there are classes for anything and everything if you choose to look.

Be prepared: Be prepared to spend the night outdoors. Have extra food, water, and clothing to make it comfortable. Be sure you can build or create a temporary structure. You might be far from help but you can keep yourself comfortable until help does arrive if you need it.

Heights: I mean, really, who isn't a *little* scared of heights? It's an evolutionary mechanism built in to protect us from falling. There have been times, however (I'm sure you can relate), where this fear is triggered when it shouldn't be. I'll be hiking along, and all of the sudden I look down or out to the horizon, and I'm paralyzed with fear:

For a long time, just *thinking* about climbing Mount Washington gave me chills and made me nauseous. A few years ago, Nick and I were in the White Mountains of New Hampshire for the first time. Reaching the top of Mount Washington (whether by car, foot, or railway) is a must do. It is the highest peak in New Hampshire and the highest in the Northeast. It is known as the "Home of the World's Worst Weather" due to the convergence of three different weather systems at its peak. Clear summits are few and far between. For some time it held the record for the highest recorded wind speed at 231 miles per hour. As anticipated, we drove up and were met with near zero visibility and a thunderstorm. We made it to the top and attempted to wait out the rain to visit the museum and weather station. After about ten minutes, we decided to make a run for it. We weren't 100 feet from the car when a lightning strike seemed to hit the ground right in front of us. We didn't say a word to one another— we both ran right back to the car. We drove down, hail pelting (and denting!) our car (in July!) and me crying the entire way to the bottom. I honestly didn't think we would make it down unharmed. Thankfully, we did, but I resolved that I would never go up there again and definitely not on foot. In fact, the entire Presidential Range was now out of the question.

Nick's cousin Norman was in from California so we traveled up to New Hampshire to see him and his parents. While planning the very short weekend, we threw around the idea of hiking the entire Presidential Traverse, Mount Jefferson, or Mount Monroe with Mount Washington. Choosing a destination or choosing between trails is an arduous task— it's a huge list of pros and cons. The Presidential Traverse was entirely too long for a day hike (22 miles and 9,000 feet gain); Mount Jefferson required more climbing than I was comfortable with. To my dismay, the trail we were researching to Mount Monroe (and then continuing on to Mount Washington) seemed to be the easiest of any option. I couldn't believe it, but I was most comfortable with the mountain that was burned into my memory as hell on earth.

We did not get as early of a start to the day as I had hoped we would. We reached the trail head at 1:00 in the afternoon, and I told Nick that it was highly unlikely we'd make it to Washington. We definitely had time to hit Mount Monroe, the fourth highest peak in New Hampshire. Nick's really into superlatives, so this helped my cause. I was not prepared for a night hike down the most formidable mountain in the Northeast.

We had an unseasonably perfect day with no storms on the horizon. The Ammonoosuc Ravine Trail runs 3.1 miles and 2,500 feet up to the Lakes of the Clouds hut (run by the AMC) which provides shelter and meals to hikers in the summer months. From there, it is another .04 miles and only 350 feet to Mount Monroe and back, and another 1.5 miles and 1,300 feet to Mount Washington. We had our work cut out for us.

The trail quickly drops you into the lush forest of the Northeast. You'd never believe me, but the woods here remind me of a rainforest. Rocks and trees are blanketed with moss and mushrooms. We passed a placard in memory of Herbert Judson Young, an eighteen year old who died from hypothermia in the area in 1928. It was nearly impossible to think that such a gorgeous area in the summer could be that unforgiving in the winter. After about a mile, we came to a T intersection with the Ammonoosuc River and beared right. The trail hugs the river for the majority of the trek up and it is an incredible treat— the water keeps you cool and comfortable. The path is covered with stray rocks and root systems, and as difficult as it might be, you have to look down to watch your footing. Just being out in the woods is incredible, but this route is so packed with natural features, it is very difficult to make good time. We often stopped to investigate the micro environments around us. The raging river drowned out the conversation as we walked.

As we turned a corner, we found a gushing waterfall with the most inviting waters I've ever seen. We wanted to stop and swim so badly but knew if we did we'd be hiking back in the dark. Reluctantly, we passed the waterfall where we were met with a series of steep rocks. At that point, we were about 1.5 miles in and barely gained any elevation, so I knew the rest of the way was going to be brutal. We all took a deep breath and got to work.

I was embarrassed by how many times I had to stop to catch my breath (both because of the cardio and the height factor). Every time we stopped, I peeked behind my shoulder. The mountains we saw from the parking lot were beginning to be at eye level. Luckily, the trail began to get more technical, so I didn't have time to worry much about the heights. The higher peaks of the Northeast all seem to follow the same format: a lovely jaunt through the woods, followed by rockier sections, followed by rock slides. The slides had excellent texture so I felt secure in my footing. There were plenty of places to rest your hands and feet as you climbed.

The rock slides were skirting small streams that dumped into various waterfalls, following the mountain to the bottom. At one point, my aching legs and fear of heights combined to create a moment of weakness. I sat down and refused to get back up. The White Mountains were laid out before my eyes, but all I could do was attempt to hold down my breakfast. After taking a breather and reminding myself that people would be envious of my current position, I stood back up and continued on my way.

On most hikes in the Northeast, the alpine zone is not a considerable part of the trail. On this trip, however, we seemed to be in the alpine zone for a long time. We had passed many hikers who all said we were nearing the Lakes of the Clouds Hut. I know many hikers say that to keep you going, but I never, ever believe them. Finally, one woman was right. After passing her, I saw a glimpse of a building. I was overjoyed— we were almost there.

We stopped at the hut to eat our lunches. There was such an energy there—— hikers of all ages were buzzing around— either getting ready for a short hike, checking in, or eating lunch. The hut gets its name from the lakes beside them and they were a nice addition to the view. The hut itself has an interesting history- after a couple of climbers perished in the extreme weather in the area in June of 1900, a shelter was built for emergencies only. Hikers, however, found this to be a welcoming spot and used the shelter for pleasure trips. In 1915, the AMC decided to build a new shelter exclusively for thru hikers. Employees hike up with food and provisions for guests on their backs.

Once appetites were satiated, we left the hut for our approach to Mount Monroe. We were incredibly close but I almost didn't summit. I had a bit of an internal struggle- I had to dig deep to keep going. We made it to the summit at 5:00 PM, and after seeing the view from Mount Monroe's vantage point, I was glad I kept at it. Mount Washington was to our left— its summit clear as glass. You could make out the trail to the top, where the weather station is located. Mount Washington is a little over 1,000 feet above Mount Monroe, but its approach and summit is all rocks. This was a stark contrast from the rest of the view— lush green mountains with trails running across them like arteries. The ridge line was so inviting. Had we had more time, I would have loved to keep going. Once we took our obligatory summit pictures, we headed down. We knew it was too late for Mount Washington, and although that stung a little bit, Mount Monroe gave us the views we wanted at 5,372 feet above sea level.

We slowly made our way down, chattering away from the excitement of the hike. There was plenty of slipping but no falling. It was pretty humorous— as soon as one of us slipped another one followed suit. I spent most of the descent on my rear end, though I wished I could slide all the way to the bottom. We passed by the waterfall and the opportunity to swim. It was getting late and chilly and the waters didn't seem nearly as inviting at this time of day.

On our final mile, it started getting dark. We made it to the car at 8:00, just as the sun slipped below the horizon. After a round of high fives, we piled into the car for the drive back to Nashua. While I have the upmost respect for Mount Washington, it no longer petrifies me. To Nick's delight, I proclaimed I'd be back.

Relief!

Thank yourself: I wouldn't try to quell this one. It's important and human to be afraid. If you're in a situation wherein you shouldn't be fearful, thank your body and mind for doing its job, but tell yourself it's a false alarm. Be confident but cautious. Nick and I went on a zip line canopy tour in the woods of West Virginia (our first trip together!) and it was so much fun. Even though I was scared of heights, I realized the odds of equipment failure were astronomically low and I gave in to the experience. We had so much fun that we returned a few weeks later with friends.

Panic attacks: They are the worst. I can usually control them at the beginning without anyone even knowing. Talking myself down usually works (I've had a lot of practice) but occasionally I just can't do it. My chest will get tight, I feel as though I can't breathe, and I'll think of the most horrendous things in the world. It's sometimes impossible to discern whether or not your body is lying to you— you don't always know when it's a false alarm.

Relief!

Thank yourself: Thank your body for doing what it should. Directly after, silently scream at yourself, because, yet again, your mind and body are lying to you. Call yourself on it. Know that there's nothing wrong. I'd like to think that if there were truly something wrong with my body that I would know it. Rely on that. Know your body. Know when something is amiss and when something isn't.

A Note:

Make sure you and your traveling partner(s) are on the same page: Especially in outdoor travel, it's imperative that you are all on the same page and they know what you know. Prime example of this: there was recently a fatal black bear attack in New Jersey. The hikers were in a fairly large group and they probably would have been able to stave off the bear they encountered: Instead of following proper bear protocol (presumably due to ignorance), they split up and ran. One fell. Guess who was fatally mauled?

Ideally, there shouldn't be a discussion about what to do if shit hits the fan. You should all know exactly what to do and act accordingly.

Let others in on your fear. I know it can be a taboo subject and perceived as an admission of weakness, but it will serve you well to tell your partners. Sometimes they can be an incredible source of strength. You can't get comfort and help when you need it if you refuse to tell anyone.

Stress in succession: It sometimes helps when things go horribly wrong on the road or trail. If you have had enough mishaps you probably want to wave the white flag. It gets to the point where you have your "fuck it" moment. And that moment can be beautiful and life changing if you let it be.

IX.
Departure and Arrival

Once we make it to our destination, I'm pretty much set. There are only three things to do:

Rent a car if we haven't done so already. Sometimes, it's better to wait, especially in a place like Colorado in the winter, where an all wheel drive vehicle is sometimes required, but not easy to reserve in advance. It once took us an hour to go to every single rental kiosk, looking for a lone Subaru. We didn't find one, but we wasted an hour.

Go to a sporting goods store to purchase bear mace and a knife. When we fly (with the exception of the recent Hawai'i trip) we only pack a carry on. We find it's easier to keep it minimal as well as the added bonus of being able to walk off of the plane and get the hell out of the airport. Because we're only taking carry ons, we can't bring things like mace and knives.

Go to a grocery store and get snacks, meals, and toiletries.

We go through our trip, both of us compromising because I am such a wuss and he is Mr. Adventure and we return home happily.

Once we're home, I try to unpack as quickly as possible. Laundry is in immediately. Here's a tip: unload your suitcase at your washing machine. It makes life a lot easier.

Once everything is washed and away in its proper place, more redundancy occurs.

First, I dump everything onto the computer—camera pictures, phone pictures, and videos.

I get everything into their proper events with corresponding dates, and make a copy of each folder on my desktop. I dump those folders onto my hard drive, then put those folders into a separate folder titled "hard drive mom's". We have two hard drives— one for easy accessibility at home, another at my mom's for safekeeping. I'll throw those on the hard drive at her house the next time I see her.

Before I unplug my hard drive, I open a file entitled "map slips". We have two maps on our walls backed by cork, with slips pinned on detailing places and dates. One is for places we want to go, the other for places we've been. When we're feeling adventurous or have cabin fever, it's so nice to look at these. It's a reminder of everywhere we've been and those places we long to see. It's so refreshing to still have such a thirst for new frontiers.

Finally, I'll order a couple of prints of the best photos that highlight the trip.

After having been so ready to go back home, in about a week, I'm ready to get back out there. It never fails— it feels like you're traveling forever when it's only been a week or two, and once you're home for a week it feels like an eternity. Even after all of the shit I go through to make it happen (or, should I say, to make it happen according to my vision), I always want to go back for more.

Part Four:
You

While the ways in which I suggest you deal with your fear of traveling may help you cope in the short term or if the worst really does happen, the bottom line is this: you're the problem. You might say that the world is a big, bad, scary place and that you have every right to be fearful. The truth is that the world has always been a scary place. Everything is violent... even the way we came to exist. The outdoors you love so much? It is chock full of death and destruction. The world is actually less dangerous than it used to be in many ways, though combing through the news would tell you otherwise. We have more access to what is going on in every corner of the world than we ever had before, so of course everything is fraught with death and violence.

Keep exploring and traveling. You won't necessarily become more comfortable, but you'll have the tools to deal with yourself. You'll start recognizing when intrusive, destructive thoughts come to mind and how to eradicate them. You'll start to learn more about yourself, and there is no better place to do it than on the road or trail. There's no running from yourself there.

If you don't change the way you perceive yourself, you'll find the next monster in the closet. Something will always stress you out or cause you to be fearful. Some people might need a little extra pharmaceutical help, but for many of us, we just need to make a conscious choice to change our outlook. Your anxieties tend to creep into your mind...they're unconscious thoughts. They seemingly appear out of nowhere. The good news is that all of the anxiety is totally and utterly contained within yourself. You've created the anxiety and you have the power to destroy it. So fucking obliterate it.

Don't make excuses. Time and money don't necessarily need to be hurdles. You can find a way to make it work if you really want to. Recognize that you're making excuses and that the real problem is you.

When you think of memories, what do you think of? Of course, most people think of their loved ones. When you call on those memories, where did they occur? Sure, there is beauty and meaning in the minutiae of day to day life, but I think most of us call on memories of when we're out and about exploring. Though it has been the prerogative of man to settle down lately, most of us long for adventure and the freedom it brings. Don't deny yourself those memories. If you want them, work to create them.

Examine the way you think about travel. I have a really bad habit of saying no immediately. If something doesn't sound like "me" I instantly want to dismiss it. Start saying yes and see where it leads you. You'd be surprised what you can do if you make the decision to just do it.

If I can rationalize my fears and make them manageable, you most certainly can. Though I've made leaps and bounds, I'm still a work in progress. But aren't we all? I've been really, really bad at my worst. Surely, you can handle it. See you on the road (or trail)!

Hey you!

Did this not help? Are there other things that you're fearful of that I didn't cover? Is your spouse or friend bugging you to join them on the trail? Do you just want to talk?

sarahdtiedemann@gmail.com
www.sarahdtiedemann.com